TAPAS

MADE EASY

TOMÁS GARCÍA

NEW HOLLAND

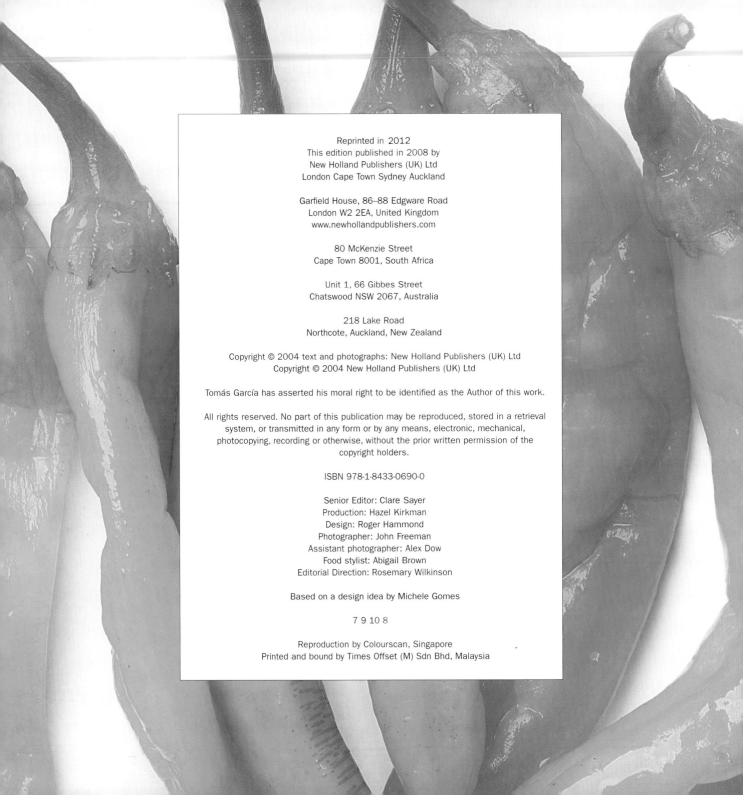

Reprinted in 2012
This edition published in 2008 by
New Holland Publishers (UK) Ltd
London Cape Town Sydney Auckland

Garfield House, 86–88 Edgware Road
London W2 2EA, United Kingdom
www.newhollandpublishers.com

80 McKenzie Street
Cape Town 8001, South Africa

Unit 1, 66 Gibbes Street
Chatswood NSW 2067, Australia

218 Lake Road
Northcote, Auckland, New Zealand

ISBN 978-1-8433-0690-0

Senior Editor: Clare Sayer
Production: Hazel Kirkman
Design: Roger Hammond
Photographer: John Freeman
Assistant photographer: Alex Dow
Food stylist: Abigail Brown
Editorial Direction: Rosemary Wilkinson

Based on a design idea by Michele Gomes

7 9 10 8

Reproduction by Colourscan, Singapore
Printed and bound by Times Offset (M) Sdn Bhd, Malaysia

ACKOWLEDGEMENTS

For Adela Lana, my mother-in-law, who has been nourishing me with love and food so generously for so long. She, and not less her sisters Josefa and Olga, has made me better appreciate the bountiful heart and soul of Spain.

Thanks also to John and Alex, who made taking technically brilliant and imaginative photos appear as normal and straightforward as buttering bread; to Clare, as organized and tolerant an editor as one could hope for; and to Abi, whose skills in bringing these recipes to life were a genuine revelation and who is already a bright star in the culinary firmament.

TAPAS

MADE EASY

CONTENTS

INTRODUCTION

It could be argued that Spain has the most civilized bar culture in the world. Tapas are fundamental to this way of life. They are those delicious morsels that appear magically next to that drink you've just ordered in any number of bars, from San Sebastian in the north, across to Santiago in the the north-west, through Madrid to Barcelona in the east and down to Seville and Granada, the Moorish south.

Spanish bars are, before anything else, welcoming. Their sophistication lies in their ability to produce and serve an entire range, from soothing comfort food to exacting haute cuisine. The local in Spain is a bar where you can have a quick breakfast on the way to work, or a couple of drinks with friends on your way home. It is where everyone, from great-grandma to the squirming infant, can enjoy a drink and some food, usually to socialize before lunch or dinner. This is family life conducted at large. The huge variety of tapas dishes means there is always something for everyone and they have a mellowing effect on those consuming alcohol – ultimately this means that the atmosphere is more relaxed and gregarious.

This book aims to introduce you to tapas you can make with confidence at home. Authentic Spanish ingredients are now available around the world, not only in specialist delicatessens, but also in ordinary supermarkets. The Spanish themselves are responding to the global village by using a much wider range of ingredients. Soy and Worcester sauces, papaya and avocado, smoked salmon, curry paste – even Maldon salt are commonplace, casually but tellingly incorporated to satisfy ever more sophisticated palates.

Spanish cooking is a rich and identifiable tradition which proudly reflects its regionalism. For every pan-Iberian staple such as the *tortilla*, or potato omelette, there are a dozen dishes particular to a locality. The variations are subtle and are the result of differing local ingredients. This book aims to reflect the typically Spanish as well as the new developments in creative tapas increasingly surfacing in modern bars. The only criteria worth acknowledging are: does it satisfy your appetite? Does it enhance and complement that drink that has delicately teased those gastric juices? With this book, I hope the answer will be yes.

HISTORY OF TAPAS

There are many theories as to the origin of tapas. Some say that this culinary tradition was invented by Alfonso X, known as the Wise, King of Castille and Leon – or rather by his chef, who treated the King's exhaustion with a daily succession of very small dishes, each helped along with a small glass of wine. His recovery was so remarkable that the old king tried to spread the news: eat little and often, he commanded, and you will live longer.

A less charming explanation for the origin of tapas is the Spanish verb *tapar*, meaning "to cover". Slices of ham or cheese were used to cover the *potes*, clay wine cups, ostensibly to keep out the flies. From these scarcely hygienic beginnings was elaborated the wondrous range of tapas we know today. Another theory is that they developed as a way of boosting energy in the middle of the day, or as a post-siesta pick-me-up.

Gradually it became clear that tapas were not only delicious and satisfying to consume but were also useful to the body in that they soaked up some of the accompanying alcohol. Olives and nuts or slices of sausage, both *salchichón* and *chorizo* styles, fish freshly fried or preserved in oil or pickled in vinegar, fried dough with all manner of flavourings, all became staples. The New World offered up its bounty, with the humble potato outstandingly affording a range of possibilities, not least of which is the always welcome potato omelette, the *tortilla*.

And it is a living tradition, reflecting the changing world, as new ingredients and small but perfectly formed fantasies are plated up before the feasting eyes and rumbling appetites of devotees. The tapa tradition, the Spaniard's drink and a bite in his local, is stronger than ever.

HOW TO SERVE TAPAS

Tapas is a general term for small snacks, defined best by being eaten comfortably standing up to accompany your drink. They come in a variety of different forms and can be anything from a handful of stuffed olives to a crisp deep-fried artichoke to a gently simmering *chorizo* stew. The recipes in this book are divided up according to how they would be served in a Spanish bar. Cocktail sticks are an essential tool in the enjoyment of tapas and are used to spear or pierce a whole range of tapas. In Spain these are known as *pinchos*, from the verb *pinchar*, meaning to prick or pierce. *Pinchos* have come to mean any tapas that are served on or with cocktail sticks and skewers. There is a whole range of tapas that are arranged in layers on toasted bread, rather like the Italian *crostini*: in Spain they are called *montados* or *tostas*, which is a better explanation of what they are. Pastry tartlets become useful "containers" – all manner of delicious ingredients can be piled into a puff pastry tart.

The joy of tapas, for most people, is that they can enjoy three or four different dishes without feeling that they are overeating. When preparing tapas, it is a good idea to create a balance of dishes and to choose items that complement and contrast with one another. Think about the sharp tang of a dish of marinated anchovies, the paprika-flavoured spicy *chorizo* or the robust flavour of a garlicky pork brochette – and work out how well these dishes work together. If you are catering for a party, don't make things too complicated for yourself and just concentrate on a few dishes. Some tapas, such as the *gildas* (see page 53) can be prepared in advance.

Tapas were developed to complement wine but they can of course be enjoyed with other drinks. Today, it is a safe bet to say that more beer than wine is drunk in Spanish bars, especially amongst younger people. In many bars you will find that it is common practice to ask for a *corto*, a wine glass of beer to drink with your *tapa*. Smaller drinks work better because of the habit of moving from bar to bar, variously called the *tapeo* or *chiquiteo*. It is a triumph of evolved social engineering: the proportion of food to alcohol is friendlier, people move around a small area full of small bars and inevitably run into familiar faces, and a large number of smaller bars are guaranteed custom, able to offer a wide or specialised range of fresh tapas cheaply to conveyor loads of customers. Instant, fluent conviviality.

Tapas also go ideally with sherry. *Jerez de la Frontera* and *Sanlúcar de Barrameda* both produce excellent wines whose nobility has been favourably compared with those of Champagne. A chilled *fino*, *oloroso* or *manzanilla* is a perfect accompaniment to the food in this book.

INGREDIENTS

Although we have become used to an ever wider selection of ingredients from around the world in our supermarkets, authentic Spanish tapas are today still based on the traditional range of ingredients that have evolved over the centuries. These are the staples which should be your starting point when planning a tapas menu at home.

Most simple of all is a handful of olives, available in the most rudimentary of bars, if only directly from a tin onto a saucer. You can do much better: olives stuffed with anchovies, pimentos, almonds, lemon, for instance, as well a wide selection of different olives in herbs, garlic, lemon and so on.

The two other ingredients of the classic tapa *gilda* (see page 53) are widely available and easily stored. The *guindilla* is a small hot chilli in vinegar and the *boqueron* is the silvery anchovy preserved in oil and vinegar, giving it a characteristically delicate flavour, quite unlike the more familiar dark salted variety.

Spaniards are justly proud of their cured ham *jamón*. The best quality is *jamón ibérico*, made from giant black pigs that traditionally graze on acorns in the extensive oak forests of Extremadura in the western area of Spain. Otherwise, you will now see *jamón serrano*, cured in exactly the same way and exported worldwide, in your local supermarkets. The Spanish do like to serve it thicker cut than the paper thin Parma of the Italians – a matter of taste.

There are many varieties of the *chorizo*, such as the magnificent mature *ibérico* version that can be sliced thick or thin, or the less cured smaller versions used for cooking, either to enliven stews and pulses or roasted in wine, crunchy and juicy.

Pimientos de piquillo are an object lesson in how a high quality ingredient can be made widely available. They are small red peppers or pimentos, char-grilled and peeled, and then marinated. This process brings out a magnificent sweet, tangy flavour, a superb complementary ingredient in many Spanish dishes.

There can be no real taste of Mediterranean cooking without olive oil. Like the grape, the apparently humble olive responds to the soil and climate it's grown in to give subtly varying, characteristic tastes, hardly any two oils identical in flavour. It is entirely possible to have a range of olive oils to hand which will fill your every need, satisfy your every culinary desire. Extra-virgin olive oil is used for dressings, its strong, fruity flavour the result of a first, cold pressing. It is justifiably expensive and its low burning threshold makes it unsuitable for hot frying. Virgin olive oil is almost always good enough for dressings, usually has a less intense flavour and can be used for hot frying. A third type, often labelled "pomace" olive oil, is pressed from the skin and stone of the olive after the first pressings. It can be very cheap and yet it still retains a very good flavour. Its high burning threshold make it ideal for frying.

The spice most prevalent in Spanish cuisine is *pimentón*, which we know as paprika. This is dried and powdered red pimento and is available as *pimentón picante* (hot) or *pimentón dulce* (mild). In some cases it may even be smoked. It's what gives *chorizo* its unmistakeable taste. No Spanish kitchen can function without garlic and its classic combination with parsley, salt and olive oil, what the French call a *persillade*, is used as a marinade, the basis for a sauce with meat or fish, or as a simple condiment for added flavour.

The Spanish love seafood and they have a huge variety of it pickled, sauced, soused, generally preserved in cans or jars. They are staples in supermarkets and are becoming more widely available outside Spain. These are so tasty, so intensely flavoured that all you need do is serve them on a tosta. *Mejillones en escabeche* (marinated mussels) are available tinned, as well as squid, octopus, clams, cockles, the humble sardine and yet more obscure molluscs. They all positively improve by being cooked and thus preserved.

Many of the recipes in this book call for prawns – I would always recommend going to your local fishmonger and buying fresh prawns, preferably with tail on. Alternatively, frozen prawns also work well and will defrost in no time.

Bacalao is an important Spanish ingredient but is not as widespread outside of Spain. There are many perfectly good alternatives, such as good, undyed smoked haddock, however, if you can get hold of it, it is worth the effort. *Bacalao* is effectively cod which has been preserved by being salted and dried. The success of salt cod depends very much on the quality of the fish more than anything else. Try to avoid buying thin, meagre pieces: the plumper the better. Before using, it needs thorough desalination – you must use plenty of water and allow at least 24 hours. Soak in clean, fresh water and change the water about three or four times, then drain and pat the piece dry. You should be able to skin the fish quite easily and there will be bones to pick out (use tweezers to remove the tiniest of these).

Below you will find a list of ingredients you should usefully have in your kitchen. Together with the fresh ingredients necessary for a particular tapa, this selection will enable you to prepare everything you will find to tempt you in this book.

STORE CUPBOARD

Good-quality sea salt

Jars of marinated seafood

English mustard powder

Extra-virgin olive oil

Light olive oil

Tinned tuna

Tinned tomatoes

Tinned petits pois

Tinned artichoke hearts

Tinned chickpeas

Green olives, pitted and/or stuffed with anchovies, pimientos, lemon etc.

Tins or jars of *pimientos de piquillo* (chargrilled ones have a better flavour)

Jars of *guindilla* chillies (small hot green chillies in vinegar)

Mild smoked paprika (*pimentón dulce*)

Hot smoked paprika (*pimentón picante*), chilli powder or cayenne pepper

Jars of tapenade (black olive paste)

Curry paste

Ground turmeric

Ground cumin

Ground coriander

Brandy or *orujo*, the equivalent of the French *marc* or Italian *grappa*, a very dry, clear eau-de-vie

Sherry vinegar

KITCHEN SHELF

Fresh garlic

Parsley plant

Coriander plant

Free-range eggs

FRIDGE

Lemons

Limes

Unsalted butter

Streaky bacon or *pancetta*

Jamón serrano

FREEZER

Frozen peas (petits pois have more flavour)

Frozen spinach

Packets of vol-au-vent cases

Ready-made puff-pastry

EQUIPMENT

As this is a book about preparing tapas easily at home, it follows that you are not going to need a lot of professional catering equipment to prepare them. However, some basic items will help make preparing these dishes as quick and as stress-free as possible.

KNIVES AND BOARDS This is your preparation world in microcosm. Add only a source of heat, and you could say all the basic equipment needs are satisfied. People can be very intense about kitchen knives – and are prepared to pay a premium to give themselves an edge (so to speak!) Good, sharp knives are important, but you do not have to pay through the nose for them. You'll manage with one small and one large knife for chopping, and a steel or carborundum block to keep them sharp. It's not helpful to chuck them into a drawer after use, as this exposure dulls the blade, so a block or a sheath is recommended. A third knife, with a serrated edge, is good for slicing softer items, such as tomatoes. A good chopping board is essential, so choose one that you feel at home with. I find wooden boards more satisfying than cold, efficient plastic. Try to keep different boards for different jobs, as a wooden board will often retain the smell of garlic and onions.

FRYING PANS The preference for fried food in Spain is reflected in a number of the recipes in this book. At least two good frying pans are necessary. Good-quality non-stick are essential, unless you have cast-iron skillets which need seasoning.

SAUCEPANS Stainless steel heavy-based saucepans are excellent, but aluminium pans with a heavy, heat-conducting base are perfectly fine. A small, spouted, heavy milk pan is also useful.

FOOD PROCESSOR OR BLENDER For the purposes of these recipes, no electric appliance is really necessary. Certain jobs are made much easier, such as chopping large quantities of herbs, making mayonnaise or aïoli, or mincing meat.

OTHER EQUIPMENT Have wooden spoons, a palette knife, a slotted spoon, a grater, heatproof tongs, a vegetable peeler, kitchen foil, various bowls and baking sheets to hand. Cocktail sticks, wooden skewers and a variety of small dishes and bowls are necessary for serving up your tapas.

COCKTAIL STICKS

TORTILLA ESPAÑOLA (SPANISH OMELETTE)

This classic potato and onion omelette must be perfectly cooked. The potatoes should never be boiled first: it doesn't save much time and adversely affects the flavour. Do not be alarmed by the amount of oil needed, as this will be strained away. Although the *tortilla* can be made hours ahead, it is best served when still warm.

makes 24 pinchos

INGREDIENTS

3 large eggs

1 large clove garlic

750 g (1 lb 11 oz) Maris Piper potatoes, peeled and cubed

500 g (1¼ lb) onions, diced

500 ml (18 fl oz) oil for frying

salt

EQUIPMENT

non-stick medium frying pan

cocktail sticks

METHOD

Break the eggs into a bowl and whisk. Finely grate the garlic into the eggs.

Mix the potatoes and onions together in a bowl. Heat the oil in the frying pan, add the potato and onion mixture then turn down the heat slightly. Season with salt and stir the mixture repeatedly, so that it does not stick to the bottom, for 10 minutes or until the potato is cooked (test a piece with a fork). Turn the mixture out into a strainer over a bowl. (Reserve the oil for another dish.) After a minute, add the mixture to the eggs and stir thoroughly.

Return the pan to the heat and add just enough of the oil to cover the base in a thin film. After 30 seconds, add the egg and potato mixture, immediately spreading it evenly around the pan. Cook over a high heat, being extremely careful not to allow it to stick to the bottom. Remove from the heat.

After 2 minutes, oil a plate and place it over the frying pan, then carefully invert the pan (over the sink) to reveal a golden brown omelette. Return the pan to the heat, adding a teaspoon of the oil. After 10 seconds, slide the *tortilla* off the plate and into the pan. Cook for a further 1 minute. Turn out on to the plate. The golden brown *tortilla* should be set, yet still soft in the centre, the potatoes crumbly.

Cut into eight segments, then cut each segment into three and serve.

TORTILLA ARNOLD BENNETT makes 24 pinchos **INGREDIENTS** 450 g (1 lb) undyed smoked haddock; 300 ml (10 fl oz) milk; 350 ml (12 fl oz) oil for frying; 450 g (1 lb) potatoes, peeled and cubed; 225 g (8 oz) onions, diced; 3 large eggs; 1 clove garlic, crushed; salt and freshly ground black pepper **METHOD** Poach the smoked haddock in the milk (almost covering it) for 5–6 minutes. Strain and set aside to cool. Beat the eggs and cook the potatoes and onions as before (see page 19). Mix together in a large bowl. Skin and flake the fish with a fork, carefully removing any bones. Fold the fish into the egg mixture, add the crushed garlic and season to taste. Cook and serve the omelette as before (see page 19).

TORTILLA WITH SMOKED SALMON makes 24 pinchos **INGREDIENTS** 350 ml (12 fl oz) oil for frying; 450 g (1 lb) potatoes, peeled and cubed; 225 g (8 oz) onions, diced; 3 large eggs; 150 g (5 oz) cream cheese; 1 large clove garlic, crushed; 200 g (7 oz) smoked salmon, cut into 5-cm (2-in) strips; freshly ground black pepper **METHOD** Cook the potatoes and onions as before (see page 19). Add the potatoes and then fold in the salmon pieces. Whisk the cream cheese into the egg mixture and fold in the salmon after the potatoes. Cook and serve the omelette as before (see page 19).

SPINACH AND CHEESE TORTILLA makes 24 pinchos **INGREDIENTS** 350 ml (12 fl oz) oil for frying; 450 g (1 lb) potatoes, peeled and cubed; 225 g (8 oz) onions, diced; 3 large eggs; 1 large clove garlic, crushed; 225 g (8 oz) spinach, drained weight (freshly wilted); 225 g (8 oz) grated Cheddar, Gruyère, Parmesan or Manchego cheese; salt and freshly ground black pepper; pinch of grated nutmeg **METHOD** Cook the potatoes and onions as before (see page 19). Beat the eggs in a large bowl and whisk in the crushed garlic. Fold the spinach and the grated cheese into the egg mixture. Add the seasoning and nutmeg and cook and serve as before (see page 19).

TORTILLA FLAMENCA makes 24 pinchos **INGREDIENTS** 2 tbsp oil; 225 g (8 oz) onions, diced; 200 g (7 oz) mushrooms, sliced; 200 g (7 oz) *jamón*, cut into 5-cm (2-in) strips; 225 g (8 oz) tinned red pimentos, drained weight, cut into strips; 225 g (8 oz) petits pois, thawed if frozen; 6 large eggs, beaten; 1 large clove garlic, crushed; salt and freshly ground black pepper **METHOD** Soften the onions in the oil for 3–4 minutes, add the mushrooms and cook for a further 5 minutes. Add the ham, stir and cook for 1 minute, before adding the pimento strips. Finally add the petits pois, stir and heat through for a minute. Season. Add the mixture to the eggs, along with the crushed garlic. Cook and serve the omelette as before (see page 19).

PATATAS BRAVAS (FIERY POTATOES)

The essence of this tapas dish of fried or roasted potatoes is the boldly piquant dipping sauce that makes them fiery and bold – in a word *bravas*. This classic sauce includes the hot *guindilla* chillies and chilli pepper. Serve this spicy *pincho* as hot as possible.

serves 10

INGREDIENTS

1 medium onion, diced

1 tbsp oil

½ bay leaf

1 *guindilla* chilli

1 tbsp flour

1 tsp hot smoked paprika, chilli powder or cayenne pepper

100 ml (3½ fl oz) water

1.5 kg (3¼ lb) Maris Piper potatoes, peeled

2 cloves garlic, crushed

salt

oil for frying

EQUIPMENT

2 frying pans

roasting tin

cocktail sticks

METHOD

Heat the oil in frying pan. Add the onion and soften over a medium heat for a couple of minutes before adding the bay leaf and *guindilla* chilli. Cook for a further 2 or 3 minutes and then sprinkle on the flour and, stirring continuously, add the hot smoked paprika. Slowly add small amounts of the water, stirring continuously, until the sauce has the consistency of runny custard. Allow to simmer very gently for 10 minutes. Pass the sauce through a sieve and return to the heat.

If you are roasting the potatoes, preheat the oven to 230˚C/450˚F/Gas Mark 8. Cut the potatoes into small chunks and place in a lightly oiled roasting tin. Mix in the garlic, sprinkle with salt and roast for 20 minutes or until crisp and golden. To fry, cut the potatoes into thickish chips or ½-cm (¼-in) slices and mix in the garlic. Season with salt. Heat the oil in a large frying pan and fry the potatoes gently until soft, increasing the heat at the end to turn them golden. Drain. Sprinkle the roasted or fried potatoes generously with the sauce and serve immediately.

PATATAS AÏOLI (POTATOES WITH GARLIC MAYONNAISE) serves 10 **INGREDIENTS** 2 large egg yolks; 3 cloves garlic, crushed; 2 tsp vinegar or lemon juice; pinch of English mustard powder (optional); 350 ml (12 fl oz) light olive oil; 2 tbsp warm water; 1.5 kg (3¼ lb) potatoes; salt and freshly ground black pepper **METHOD** Put the egg yolks, garlic, vinegar or lemon juice, mustard, salt and pepper in a blender or food processor and whizz briefly. With the motor running, very slowly trickle in the oil until the mixture thickens and emulsifies. Add the water at the end. Cook the potatoes as before (see page 23), slather with the aïoli and serve immediately.

NOTE: If you prefer not to make your own aïoli, grate or crush the garlic into good-quality bought mayonnaise for equally successful results.

PATATAS AIOLI ESTRAGON (POTATOES WITH TARRAGON MAYONNAISE) serves 10 **INGREDIENTS** 2 large egg yolks; 2 tsp vinegar or lemon juice; pinch of English mustard powder (optional); 350 ml (12 fl oz) light olive oil; 2 tbsp warm water, 1 tbsp chopped fresh tarragon, 1.5 kg (3¼ lb) potatoes; salt and freshly ground black pepper **METHOD** Cook the potatoes, as before. Prepare the mayonnaise as above, omitting the garlic. Stir in the chopped fresh tarragon and serve.

PATATAS EN SALSA VERDE (POTATOES WITH PARSLEY AND GARLIC) serves 10 **INGREDIENTS** 1 bunch fresh parsley, finely chopped; 3 cloves garlic, crushed; 3 tbsp olive oil; 1 tbsp vinegar or lemon juice (optional); 1.5 kg (3¼ lb) potatoes; salt and pepper **METHOD** To make the *persillade*, mix together the parsley, garlic, olive oil and vinegar or lemon juice if using and warm through. (If you prefer, keep the garlic cloves whole and pound to a paste in a mortar, add the chopped parsley, pound further then add the oil.) Fry or roast the potatoes as before (see page 23), pour over the *persillade* dressing, mixing to coat thoroughly, and serve immediately.

CROQUETAS DE PESCADO (FISH CROQUETTES)

Classic croquetas (croquettes) are made with a stiff bechamel sauce as the base. A far easier and equally delicious alternative is to use mashed potato. These croquetas are effectively mini fishcakes.

makes 20

INGREDIENTS

450 g (1 lb) floury potatoes,
    e.g. King Edward

500 g (1 lb 2 oz) fish of your choice,
    e.g. cod, haddock, hake, salmon etc.

300 ml (10 fl oz) milk or fish stock

1 large onion, finely diced

2 cloves garlic

1 tsp hot smoked paprika

1 bunch fresh parsley, finely chopped

1 tbsp light olive oil

3 large eggs

salt and freshly ground black pepper

1–2 tbsp flour

2–3 tbsp fine breadcrumbs

350 ml (12 fl oz) oil for frying

EQUIPMENT

cocktail sticks

2 large frying pans

METHOD

Boil the potatoes then drain and mash, adding nothing to them yet. Gently poach the fish in milk or fish stock (the latter is best for salmon), bringing to a simmer for about 3–4 minutes. Allow the fish to cool, then remove any skin and bones and flake with a fork. Soften the onion in the olive oil for 3–4 minutes before adding the garlic and paprika. Beat one of the eggs in a bowl and add to it the flaked fish, onion and parsley. Season generously and then carefully fold the mixture into the potatoes. Making sure the fish keeps its shape, take small tablespoonfuls of the mixture and form into balls. Coat in flour. Whisk the remaining eggs, with a little milk if you like. Roll the balls first in the egg and then the breadcrumbs. Shallow-fry the croquetas in hot oil until crisp and golden. Serve with aïoli or salsa rosa (see page 74), if liked.

VARIATION CROQUETA DE BACALAO makes 20 **INGREDIENTS** 450 g (1 lb) floury potatoes; 1 tbsp mustard; 450 g (1 lb) *bacalao* (see page 13) or smoked haddock; 300 ml (10 fl oz) milk; 1 bunch fresh parsley, finely chopped; 1 tsp mustard; 3 large eggs; salt and freshly ground black pepper; 1–2 tbsp flour; 2–3 tbsp fine breadcrumbs; 350 ml (12 fl oz) oil for frying **METHOD** Make the mashed potato as above, adding the mustard. Poach and prepare the fish as above. Add the fish and parsley to one beaten egg, then fold into the mashed potatoes and continue as above.

CEVICHE DE SALMON (MARINATED SALMON)

A traditional recipe in Andalusia and coastal Latin America, this is thinly sliced raw fish soused in a marinade, usually citrus-based, for varying periods, according to taste. The acidity in the marinade "cooks" the fish. This is, of course, basic pickling, but makes a delightfully light and fresh recipe for immediate consumption.

serves 10

INGREDIENTS

450 g (1 lb) salmon fillet, skinned (monkfish, halibut or turbot are also excellent for this)

1 medium red onion, very thinly sliced

juice of 2 lemons

1 tbsp light olive oil

½ tsp hot smoked paprika, chilli powder or cayenne pepper

1 hot red chilli, finely chopped

2–3 tbsp chopped fresh parsley, coriander or chives

20 cherry tomatoes, halved

1 small pepper, deseeded and cut into 2-cm (1-in) triangles

salt and freshly ground black pepper

EQUIPMENT

sharp cook's knife

non-metallic dish

cocktail sticks

METHOD

Wrap the salmon in foil or clingfilm and put in the freezer for up to 1 hour. This makes slicing the fish much easier. Slice the fish very thinly, using a good sharp knife.

In a shallow, wide non-metallic dish, place the fish, lemon juice, oil, paprika and chilli. Season generously then add the fish, turning to coat all over. Leave to marinate in the fridge if you wish, for minutes or for several hours, depending how 'rare' you want the fish. This will also depend on how thinly you have sliced it. Add your choice of herb minutes before you assemble the *pincho*. Sandwich one or two slices of the fish between a tomato half and a pepper triangle and serve immediately.

CEVICHE TRES MARES (THREE-SEAS CEVICHE) serves 10 **INGREDIENTS** 1 large onion, thinly sliced; 450 g (1 lb) monkfish, sliced into 4-cm (2-in) pieces; 1 red chilli, seeded and diced; water from 1 fresh coconut; juice of 4 limes; 100 ml (4 fl oz) extra-virgin olive oil; 1 bunch fresh parsley, chopped; 1 avocado, cut into cubes; 20 cherry tomatoes **METHOD** Place a layer of onion and then a layer of the fish in a large shallow dish. Sprinkle with some diced chilli. Repeat these layers, finishing with a layer of onion. Drain the water from the coconut and strain it. Add to the fish with the lime juice, making sure the liquid reaches the top. Stir gently, cover and leave for at least 6 hours, or overnight if the fish is thickly sliced. Lift the fish from the marinade and pat dry on kitchen paper. Transfer to a dish, add the olive oil and herbs and stir thoroughly, leaving it to stand for at least an hour. Assemble the pincho by threading the avocado, fish and tomato onto cocktail sticks.

CEVICHE DE VIEIRA (SCALLOP CEVICHE) makes 12 **INGREDIENTS** juice of 2–3 lemons or 3–4 limes; juice of 1–2 oranges or 4 mandarins; 2 tbsp *orujo* or brandy; 12 scallops or 6 very large scallops halved horizontally; salt and pepper; ½ tsp ground cumin (optional); 250 g (9 oz) cherry tomatoes, halved **METHOD** Mix the citrus juices with the orujo or brandy and pour over the scallops. Season, adding cumin if desired, and leave to marinate for at least 3 hours. Add the tomatoes to the liquid for a few minutes before assembling the pincho by threading a tomato then a scallop and finally another tomato on to cocktail sticks. **NOTE:** Use only the freshest scallops you can find for this ceviche.

CEVICHE DE GAMBAS (PRAWN CEVICHE) makes about 20 **INGREDIENTS** 700 g (1½ lb) fresh or frozen raw prawns (see note); 1 medium red onion, finely chopped; 2 cloves garlic, crushed; juice of 2 lemons or 2 tbsp sherry vinegar; 1 small bunch fresh parsley, finely chopped; salt and pepper; 100 ml (4 fl oz) extra-virgin olive oil **METHOD** Rinse the prawns and pat dry with kitchen paper. Shell fresh prawns. Cut through the underside of each prawn, devein and press flat to make a "butterfly". Lay the prawns out in a wide, low dish and coat them with the mixture of the onion, garlic, lemon juice or vinegar, parsley, salt and pepper. Cover and leave to marinate overnight. An hour before serving, drain off the marinade and pour on the olive oil. Thread on to skewers and serve. **NOTE:** I always soak thawed prawns for about 30 minutes in 500 ml (18 fl oz) very cold water in which 2 tbsp sea salt have been dissolved. This will refresh them and firm up the flesh.

SARDINAS FRITAS (FRIED SARDINES)

Sardines are often cooked whole in Spain, but here it is best to gut them. With a very sharp, pointed knife, in one movement cut through from behind the head down along the edge of the belly.

makes 10

INGREDIENTS

10 sardines, not longer than
   15–20 cm (6–8 in)

350 ml (12 fl oz) oil for frying

2 tbsp flour

salt

freshly ground black pepper

1 large lemon, quartered

EQUIPMENT

sharp knife

heavy-based frying pan

METHOD

Heat the oil in a heavy-based frying pan, large enough to take 2 or 3 sardines. When the oil is hot – 180°C (350°F) – a small cube of bread dropped into it sizzles immediately and browns in 20 seconds. Put the flour in a plastic bag and season with the salt and pepper. Drop the sardines into the bag and shake well to coat, Lift out, shaking off excess flour. Fry the sardines in the hot oil for 1–2 minutes on each side. Squeeze over the juice from the lemon wedges.

NOTE: To give the fish a characteristically Spanish tang, add 2 tsp hot smoked paprika or chilli powder to the flour. For a Moorish flavour, add 1 tsp of each of ground turmeric and ground cumin to the flour.

SARDINETAS FRITAS (FRIED SPRATS) makes about 20 pinchos **INGREDIENTS** 450 g (1 lb) fresh sprats; 500 ml (18 fl oz) milk; 2 tbsp flour, seasoned with salt and freshly ground black pepper; 350 ml (12 fl oz) oil for frying; 1 large lemon, quartered **METHOD** Soak the cleaned fish in milk for at least 10 minutes then pat dry on kitchen paper. Dust with the seasoned flour and deep-fry them in hot oil as above. Serve sprinkled with lemon juice, to be speared with cocktail sticks. **NOTE:** sprats can be fried and eaten whole, but, like sardines, are easily cleaned.

CHANQUETES (WHITEBAIT)

makes about 20 pinchos **INGREDIENTS** 450 g (1 lb) frozen whitebait; 500 ml (18 fl oz) milk; 2 tbsp flour, seasoned with salt and freshly ground black pepper; 350 ml (12 fl oz) oil for frying; 1 large lemon, quartered **METHOD** Defrost the fish thoroughly and soak in the milk for 10 minutes. Dust with seasoned flour and fry and serve as above.

ALBONDIGAS (VEAL AND PORK MEATBALLS)

makes about 24

INGREDIENTS

750 g (1½ lb) veal mince

250 g (9 oz) pork mince

2 cloves garlic, crushed

1 small bunch fresh parsley, chopped

150 ml (5 fl oz) milk

5 tbsp stale breadcrumbs

3 medium onions, finely diced

2 tbsp light olive oil

1 tbsp flour

125 ml (4 fl oz) white wine

salt and freshly ground black pepper

½ tsp grated nutmeg

2 large eggs, whisked

flour for dusting

250 ml (8 fl oz) oil for frying

METHOD

Mix the meats together in a bowl, adding the garlic and parsley and set aside. Pour the milk on to the breadcrumbs. Heat the oil in a pan and soften the onion for 4–5 minutes, sprinkle over the flour, stirring continuously, then add the wine and seasoning. Bring to a simmer, then reduce the heat to very low, cooking and stirring for 15–20 minutes. Pass through a sieve and set aside in a casserole. Season the meat with salt, pepper and nutmeg. Squeeze the excess milk from the breadcrumbs and add to the meat, together with the eggs and three tablespoons of the sauce. Mix thoroughly. Roll the mixture into small balls, then dust with the flour. Heat the oil in a frying pan and fry the meatballs for 5–6 minutes, until lightly brown. Remove, drain and transfer to the casserole. Poach the meatballs gently in the sauce for 30–40 minutes, until they are tender and the sauce is very thick. Serve warm.

VARIATION: ALBONDIGAS DE POLLO (CHICKEN MEATBALLS) makes 24 **INGREDIENTS** 900 g (2 lb) chicken breasts, diced; 150 g (5 oz) streaky bacon, diced; 3 cloves garlic, crushed; 1 bunch fresh parsley, chopped; 100 g(4 oz) olives, diced; 150 ml (5 fl oz) milk; 5 tbsp stale breadcrumbs; 2 onions, diced; 2 tsp light olive oil; 1 large egg, beaten; salt and pepper; flour for dusting; 250 ml (8 fl oz) oil for frying; 400 g (14 oz) tinned chopped tomatoes; 125 ml (4 fl oz) white wine; 1 bay leaf; 250 ml (8 fl oz) chicken stock **METHOD** Put the chicken, bacon, half the garlic, half the parsley and olives in a food processor. Whizz briefly. Pour the milk on to the breadcrumbs, squeeze out the excess milk and add to the meat, with one onion, softened in the olive oil and the egg. Season. Mix and form into balls, dust with flour and fry as above. Transfer to a casserole. Pour off all but 1 tablespoon of the oil and use this to soften the other onion for 4–5 minutes, add the tomatoes, remaining garlic and parsley, wine and bay leaf. Simmer for 10 minutes before adding the stock. Add the meatballs to the sauce and simmer gently for 30 minutes. Serve warm.

HUEVOS RELLENOS (STUFFED EGGS)

Stuffed eggs are always popular. Hard-boiled and halved, their yolks removed and mixed with mayonnaise and a variety of, usually sharp, ingredients to counterbalance the blandness of the whites, they lend themselves to all manner of variations.

makes 24

INGREDIENTS

12 small eggs

6 tbsp mayonnaise

1 tsp mustard

salt and freshly ground black pepper

6 cherry tomatoes

6 leaves lollo rosso lettuce, torn into
    4-cm (1½-in) pieces

EQUIPMENT

saucepan

cocktail sticks

METHOD

Hard-boil the eggs, peel and cut in half lengthways. Scoop out the yolks and mash them together with the mayonnaise and mustard. Season well. Heap the mixture back into the egg halves. Top with a tomato half and a piece of lettuce and serve with cocktail sticks with which to spear the egg halves.

TUNA-STUFFED EGGS

makes 24 **INGREDIENTS** 12 small eggs; 6 tbsp mayonnaise; 1 tsp mustard; salt and freshly ground black pepper; 1 x 185 g (7 oz) tin good-quality tuna; fresh parsley, to garnish **METHOD** Prepare the eggs as before (see page 37). Drain the tuna and flake; add to the mayonnaise mixture and heap the mixture back into the egg halves. Serve garnished with parsley.

STUFFED EGGS WITH HAM

makes 24 **INGREDIENTS** 12 small eggs; 6 tbsp mayonnaise; 1 tsp mustard; salt and freshly ground black pepper; 115 g (4 oz) jamón **METHOD** Prepare the eggs as before (see page 37). Cut 24 strips of jamón, 5 x 1 cm (2 x ¼ in) and set aside. Dice the remaining jamón, add to the mayonnaise mixture and proceed as above, covering each stuffed egg with a strip of jamón before.

STUFFED EGGS WITH CRAB

makes 24 **INGREDIENTS** 12 small eggs; 6 tbsp
mayonnaise; 1 tsp mustard; salt and freshly ground black
pepper; 1 small tin crabmeat; fresh parsley, to garnish
METHOD Prepare the eggs as before (see page 37). Add
the flaked crabmeat to the mayonnaise mixture and heap
back into the egg halves. Garnish with parsley and serve.

STUFFED EGGS WITH CAPERS AND GHERKINS

makes 24 **INGREDIENTS** 12 small eggs; 6 tbsp
mayonnaise; 1 tsp mustard; salt and freshly ground black
pepper; 1 tbsp chopped capers and 1 tbsp chopped
gherkins **METHOD** Prepare the eggs as before (see page
37). Add the capers and gherkins to the mayonnaise
mixture, heap back into the egg halves and serve.

COLIFLOR REBOZADA (CAULIFLOWER FRITTERS)

A teaspoon of dry yeast added to the batter for these crisp and golden fritters ensures they puff up to an irresistible lightness.

makes about 24

INGREDIENTS

1 large cauliflower, cut into florets

350 ml (12 fl oz) oil for frying

2 lemons, quartered

FOR THE BATTER:

150 ml (5 fl oz) milk

3 tbsp white wine

3 tbsp oil

1 large egg, separated

1 tsp dry yeast

about 250 g (9 oz) flour

salt

EQUIPMENT

large, wide frying pan

slotted spoon

cocktail sticks

METHOD

First make the batter by putting the milk, wine, oil, egg yolk, yeast and a teaspoon of salt into a bowl. Stir well with a wooden spoon and start adding the flour, little by little, stirring continuously until you achieve a batter the consistency of single cream. You may need less flour. Set aside in a warm place to rest for half an hour.

Trim the stalks of the cauliflower florets and place in a large pan of boiling salted water. Bring back to the boil and simmer for 1–2 minutes – they should not be overcooked. Drain and refresh in cold water. Set out to dry on a tea towel. Heat the oil in a large, wide frying pan suitable for deep-frying and test the temperature by dropping in a cube of bread into the oil. When the oil is the correct temperature, about 180°C (350°F), it should turn golden in about 20 seconds. Whisk the egg white to a stiff peak and fold it into the batter. This must be done at the last moment. One by one, coat the florets in the batter on a spoon and drop into the oil to deep-fry in batches of no more than five. When golden, remove with a slotted spoon and drain on kitchen paper. Keep warm while you fry the rest. Squeeze over the juice from the lemon wedges and serve immediately.

VARIATION: ALCACHOFAS REBOZADAS (ARTICHOKE FRITTERS) makes about 24 **INGREDIENTS** batter as above; 1 x 400 g (14 oz) tin artichoke hearts; 500 ml (18 fl oz) oil for frying; 2 lemons, quartered **METHOD** Drain the artichokes, cut into medium dice and season. Heat the oil as above. Dip each piece of artichoke in the batter and fry one by one, leaving enough space to allow it to puff up. Drain and keep warm. Serve at once with lemon.

CROQUETAS DE GAMBAS (PRAWN CROQUETTES)

Croquetas are ubiquitous in Spain, although they most likely originate from the French "croquettes". Their beauty lies in the bechamel base which is then mixed with your particular ingredient of choice to gives it a characteristic flavour. The possibilities are almost endless – here I have used prawns.

makes about 36

INGREDIENTS

100 g (3½ oz) butter

125 g (4 oz) plain flour

750 ml (1¼ pints) cold milk

salt and pepper

400 g (14 oz) cooked peeled prawns, diced

2 tsp tomato purée

5 or 6 tbsp fine breadcrumbs

2 large eggs, beaten

oil for deep-frying

METHOD

Melt the butter in a medium saucepan and add the flour, stirring continuously. Allow the flour to cook in the butter for a couple of minutes, continuing to stir. Start adding the cold milk little by little, stirring all the while until you have a thick, smooth sauce. Add the prawns, season well and stir in the tomato paste. Continue to cook for 7 or 8 minutes. The end result should be quite thick. It is essential that the mixture is allowed to cool completely – overnight is best.

Take a scant tablespoon of the mixture and form into a *croqueta*, a 3-4 cm (1½–2 in) cylinder. Roll the *croqueta* in the breadcrumbs, then coat in the beaten egg, then roll in the breadcrumbs again. Make sure the breadcrumbs are always dry to ensure an even coating.

Heat the oil for deep-frying in a large, heavy-based pan until the temperature reaches 180°C (350°F) or a cube of bread turns golden brown in 20–30 seconds. Fry in batches of no more than 3 or 4 for about 5 minutes until golden brown. Remove with a slatted spoon, drain on kitchen paper and serve immediately. Salsa rosa (see page 74) is a good accompaniment.

VARIATION: CROQUETAS DE JAMON (HAM CROQUETTES) makes about 36 **INGREDIENTS** 100 g (3½ oz) butter; 125 g (4 oz) plain flour; 750 ml (24 fl oz) cold milk; salt and pepper; 200 g (7 oz) *jamón*, cut into strips; 5 or 6 tbsp fine breadcrumbs; 2 large eggs, beaten; oil for deep-frying **METHOD** as above, but substitute *jamón* instead of the cooked prawns.

CHORIZO AL VINO (CHORIZO IN RED WINE)

Chorizo can be eaten at various stages of maturity. For the purposes of roasting it in red wine, the *chorizo* should be quite fresh, only slightly cured. This type of *chorizo* is available in supermarkets and is usually 10–12 cm (4–5 in) long. It is roasted whole.

serves 10

INGREDIENTS

10 *chorizo* sausages

400 ml (14 fl oz) robust red wine

METHOD

Preheat the oven to 200°C/400°F/Gas Mark 6.

Put the *chorizo* sausages into a roasting pan and pour the wine over. Roast in the hot oven for about 40 minutes.

The sausages should be browned and slightly crispy, the wine all but evaporated.

Cut each *chorizo* into 3 or 4 pieces and serve hot.

SKEWERS

PINCHOS MORUNOS (PORK BROCHETTES)

At any village fiesta throughout Spain *pinchos morunos*, a spicy legacy of the Moors, are grilled and sold in the street to revellers. This version uses pork, although the original recipe calls for lamb.

makes about 20

INGREDIENTS

900 g (2 lb) loin of pork, cut into
    2-cm (¾-in) cubes

50 ml (2 fl oz) white wine

50 ml (2 fl oz) light olive oil

3 large cloves garlic, crushed

2 tsp hot smoked paprika, chilli
    powder or cayenne pepper (or 1 tsp
    of hot smoked paprika, chilli
    powder or cayenne pepper and
    1 tsp mild smoked paprika, if you
    prefer)

½ bay leaf, crumbled

2 tsp chopped fresh thyme

salt and freshly ground black pepper

2 lemons, quartered (optional)

EQUIPMENT

non-metallic dish

griddle or grill

20 skewers

METHOD

Arrange the meat in a wide, shallow, non-metallic dish. Mix together all the other ingredients, except the lemons, and season. Pour the mixture over the meat, cover and leave to marinate, preferably in the fridge, for at least 8 hours, turning once or twice. Thread three cubes onto each skewer and cook on a very hot griddle or grill, turning once or twice, for about 8 minutes. The meat will be charred slightly, but still juicy. Squeeze over the juice of the lemon wedges, if you wish, and serve hot.

PINCHO DE CORDERO (LAMB BROCHETTES) makes about 20 **INGREDIENTS** 900 g (2 lb) lamb neck fillet, cut into 2-cm (¾-in) cubes; 50 ml (2 fl oz) white wine; 50 ml (2 fl oz) light olive oil; ½ tsp chilli powder or cayenne pepper; ½ tsp ground cumin; ½ tsp turmeric; ½ tsp ground coriander; ½ tsp ground ginger; 3 cloves garlic, crushed; salt and pepper; 2 lemons, quartered (optional) **METHOD** Combine all the ingredients for the marinade and cover the lamb pieces. Leave to marinate for at least 8 hours. Thread the meat onto skewers and cook under a hot grill, turning once or twice, for about 8 minutes. Serve hot, with the quartered lemons. **NOTE:** This is the original lamb recipe which uses traditional Moorish spices.

PINCHO DE POLLO (CHICKEN BROCHETTES) makes about 20 **INGREDIENTS** 900 g (2 lb) chicken or turkey breast, cut into 2-cm (¾-in) cubes; 50 ml (2 fl oz) light olive oil; 3 cloves garlic, crushed; 1 small bunch fresh parsley, chopped; salt and pepper; 2 lemons **METHOD** Mix together the olive oil, garlic, chopped parsley, salt and pepper and the juice of half a lemon to make a *persillade*. Marinate the meat in the persillade for 1–2 hours. Cook as above, although white meat needs a minute or two less on the griddle or grill. Serve with the remaining lemon cut into wedges.

PINCHO DE HIGADO Y BACON (CALF'S LIVER AND BACON BROCHETTES) makes about 20 **INGREDIENTS** 250 g (9 oz) streaky bacon, cut into 2-cm (¾-in) squares; 750 g (¾ lb) calf's liver, cut into 2-cm (¾-in) cubes; salt and pepper; 2 tbsp light olive oil; 2 lemons, quartered (optional) **METHOD** Thread bacon and liver pieces alternately onto the skewers. Season (be particularly generous with the pepper), sprinkle with the oil and cook on a very hot griddle or grill for about 10 minutes, turning once. Alternatively, roast in the oven, on a lightly oiled baking tray, at 200°C/400°F/Gas Mark 6, for 15–20 minutes, turning once. Squeeze lemon juice over and serve. **NOTE:** If calf's liver is unavailable, or too expensive an option, use pig's liver instead, steeped in milk for 3–4 hours to tenderize it.

BROCHETAS DE GAMBAS Y BACON (PRAWN AND BACON BROCHETTES)

The Spanish love bacon, which they cure and air-dry in the same way as their heavenly *jamón*. The combination of bacon and prawns is inspired and very popular. Packets of very thinly sliced *jamón serrano* are widely available in supermarkets.

makes 12

INGREDIENTS

150 g (5 oz) *jamón* or thinly
    sliced bacon

24 medium to large uncooked,
    headless prawns, peeled

freshly ground black pepper

1 tbsp light olive oil

2 lemons, quartered

EQUIPMENT

griddle or grill

baking tray

12 skewers

METHOD

Cut the *jamón* into pieces which will wrap generously round the prawns. Place the wrapped prawns down flat on a board and skewer them through the fattest part and the tail, making sure the *jamón* is firmly fixed. Season generously and drizzle with the oil. On a high heat, griddle, grill or barbecue the prawn and bacon brochettes for 2–3 minutes on each side, so the *jamón* crisps up. Alternatively, roast in a hot oven (220°C/425°F/Gas Mark 7) on an oiled baking tray for 8–10 minutes. Squeeze over the juice of the lemon wedges and serve immediately.

VARIATION: BROCHETAS DE RAPE Y BACON (MONKFISH AND BACON BROCHETTES) makes 12 **INGREDIENTS** 700 g (1½ lb) monkfish, halibut or turbot, cut into 2-cm (¾-in) medallions; 150 g (5 oz) *jamón* or thinly sliced bacon; 24 button mushrooms; freshly ground black pepper; 1 tbsp light olive oil; 2 lemons, quartered **METHOD** Wrap a fish medallion in a *jamón* slice, cutting off the excess. Press flat gently. Thread the *jamón*-wrapped fish medallions alternating with the mushrooms onto the skewers. Season generously with pepper and drizzle with the oil. Cook and serve as above.

GILDAS
(ANCHOVY, OLIVE AND GUINDILLA STICKS)

Gilda means lollipop, and the classic *gilda* is a simple assembly of a *guindilla* chilli (see page 12), an anchovy and an olive. The combination of good-quality pinkish anchovies, smallish, crisp, unwrinkled chillies and a freshly pitted olive produce a sophisticated mélange. The idea has been taken further in the variations on the following pages to include very different 'lollipops', none strictly a *gilda*, but all retaining the idea of a delight on a stick.

makes about 12

INGREDIENTS

100 g (3½ oz) marinated
    anchovies in olive oil
285 g (10 oz) *guindilla* chillies, cut
    into 2-cm (¾-in) pieces
225 g (8 oz) pitted green olives

EQUIPMENT

12 cocktail sticks

METHOD

Curl up each anchovy and thread it onto a cocktail stick, along with two or three *guindilla* chillies and an olive. Stack the *gilda* onto a plate and serve immediately.

NOTE: Marinated anchovies are available from specialist shops and from the delicatessen counter of most good supermarkets. They are also available tinned and in jars but the fatter, paler ones are best.

BANDERILLA TRADICIONAL (CLASSIC SKEWER) makes 12

INGREDIENTS 185 g (7 oz) tinned best-quality white tuna; 3 tomatoes, sliced in four laterally; 3 large eggs, hard-boiled and sliced in four; 12 good-quality anchovy fillets; 3 medium potatoes, boiled and sliced in four; *vinagreta* (see page 74); 12 pitted or stuffed green olives **METHOD** Layer a flake of tuna, a slice of egg, then of tomato and finally an anchovy onto a potato slice. Dress with a teaspoon of *vinagreta*. Thread an olive onto the cocktail stick and skewer the stick into the assembly.

CHAMPIÑON, GAMBA, IBERICO (MUSHROOM, PRAWN AND JAMON STICKS) makes 12 **INGREDIENTS** 12 button mushrooms, stalks removed; 50 ml (2 fl oz) light olive oil; juice of ½ lemon; 1 large clove garlic, crushed; 12 cooked prawns, peeled; 50 g (2 oz) *jamón*, cut into strips; 75 ml (3 fl oz) dry white wine; 1 tbsp finely chopped fresh parsley **METHOD** Simmer the mushrooms in plenty of salted water, adding 2 tsp of the oil and the lemon juice, for 7–8 minutes. Drain and allow to cool. Heat the remaining oil and fry the garlic until golden. Arrange the mushrooms on a serving dish and sprinkle with the wine. Thread a prawn and a strip of *jamón* onto a cocktail stick before spearing the mushroom. Pour over the garlic-flavoured oil and sprinkle with the parsley. **NOTE:** Spanish cooks add *refrito* – finely diced garlic fried in olive oil – as a finish to many simple dishes, often soups and pulses. It gives an aromatic flavour boost to otherwise bland fare.

BOQUERONES EN VINAGRETA (MARINATED ANCHOVY STICKS)

makes 12 **INGREDIENTS** 36 marinated anchovies (*boquerones*); 12 pimento-, almond- or lemon-stuffed olives; 1 large clove garlic, crushed; 1 tbsp extra-virgin olive oil; 2 tsp finely chopped fresh parsley **METHOD** Thread three folded marinated anchovies onto a cocktail stick, followed by an olive. Mix together the garlic, olive oil and parsley and drizzle over the anchovies.

GILDA FRUTOS DEL MAR (SEAFOOD STICKS) makes 12 **INGREDIENTS**

115 g (4 oz) tinned mussels in *escabeche* (see page 13); 1 x 285-g (10-oz) jar *guindilla* chillies; 1 x 285-g (10-oz) jar seafood in oil and vinegar **METHOD** Assemble a morsel or two of the seafood, followed by two or three small *guindilla* chillies and finally a plump mussel.
NOTE: Seafood in oil and vinegar, often labelled "antipasto", is available in supermarkets.

BROCHETAS DE AHUMADO CON FRUTA (SMOKED FISH AND FRUIT BROCHETTES)

Smoked salmon is now ubiquitous in Spain, particularly in the cities. Less in evidence is traditional *bacalao* (salt cod), for which smoked mackerel is a substitute here.

makes 12

INGREDIENTS

200 g (7 oz) smoked salmon

200 g (7 oz) smoked trout

200 g (7 oz) smoked mackerel

6 cherry tomatoes, halved

12 mixed green and red grapes,
   halved and deseeded

2 kiwi fruit, peeled and cut into 2-cm
   (¾-in) pieces

250 g (9 oz) assorted berries
   (strawberries, raspberries etc.)

6 green olives, pitted and halved

freshly ground black pepper

1 lemon, quartered

EQUIPMENT

12 skewers

METHOD

Cut the fish into 3–4 cm (1–1½ in) pieces. Alternate pieces of the three fish, folding where necessary, with the cherry tomatoes, fruit and olives. Season lightly with pepper and squeeze over the juice from the lemon wedges.

TOSTAS

ANCHOAS CON PATE DE OLIVAS (TOAST WITH ANCHOVIES AND BLACK OLIVE PASTE)

Many tapas are served on toasted baguette slices, the crispness of the bread offsetting the unctuousness of the topping. This recipe is a particularly delicious combination of sweet-sour marinated anchovies with pungent black olive paste.

makes 12

INGREDIENTS

1 baguette

oil for brushing

2 tbsp tapenade (black olive paste)

12–24 marinated anchovies

   (*boquerones*, see page 12)

1 tbsp extra-virgin olive oil

3 tbsp *vinagreta* (see page 74)

METHOD

Slice the baguette into rounds about 1 cm (½ in) thick and brush with a little oil. Place on a baking tray and bake in the oven for about 5 minutes, or until golden brown.

Spread the toasted bread slices with a little tapenade. Remove the anchovies from their marinade and drizzle with the olive oil. Place one or two anchovies, depending on their size, on each toasted bread slice. Add a little more tapenade and drizzle over a little *vinagreta*.

NOTE: You can experiment with all manner of ingredients to make your own tostas. Try slices of hard-boiled egg with marinated artichokes and sun-dried tomatoes, or *pimientos de piquillo* stuffed with crabmeat and mayonnaise.

MONTADO CASA VERGARA (SEAFOOD TOASTS)

An astonishing amount can be layered onto a single tosta to make extremely rich little morsels. The Basque region is particularly famous for its ambition in these elaborations, apparently marvels of construction as much as cuisine. I first tasted this in a bar in San Sebastian.

makes 12

INGREDIENTS

1 baguette

oil, for brushing

2 tbsp mayonnaise

200 g (7 oz) smoked salmon or trout

12 marinated anchovies (*boquerones*)

3 tbsp *vinagreta* (see page 74)

24 small prawns

EQUIPMENT

baking tray

METHOD

Slice the baguette into rounds about 1 cm (½ in) thick and brush with a little oil. Place on a baking tray and bake in the oven for about 5 minutes or until golden brown.

Spread the toasted bread slices with a little of the mayonnaise. Layer the smoked fish and marinated anchovies, dress with the *vinagreta*, arrange a couple of the prawns and top it all off with a little mayonnaise.

NOTE: Marinated anchovies are available from large supermarkets and good delicatessens.

BERENJENA MONTADA (AUBERGINE AND WILD MUSHROOM STACKS) makes 12 **INGREDIENTS** 1 baguette, sliced; oil, for brushing; 2 tbsp flour; salt and freshly ground black pepper; 2 narrow aubergines, cut into 24 thin slices; 2 eggs, beaten; 100 ml (4 fl oz) oil for frying; 100 g (3½ oz) *jamón*; 12 small wild mushrooms (e.g. morels); 6 *pimientos de piquillo* (see page 12); 100 ml (4 fl oz) light olive oil **METHOD** Bake the baguette slices in the oven (see page 61). Sprinkle the flour onto a plate and season. Dust the aubergine slices in the flour, dip them in the beaten egg and fry in hot oil. Drain on kitchen paper and set aside. In batches, fry the *jamón*, mushrooms and pimientos de piquillo in the light olive oil over a medium heat. Layer an aubergine slice, half a *pimiento*, mushroom, a little *jamón* and finally another aubergine slice onto each toasted bread slice.

TXITXARRO (MACKEREL AND LEEK TOASTS) makes 12 **INGREDIENTS** 1 baguette, sliced; oil, for brushing; 1 medium mackerel, cleaned and gutted; 1 medium leek, finely sliced; 1 medium onion, peeled and finely sliced; 2 tbsp light olive oil; 1 bay leaf; 100 ml (4 fl oz) dry white wine; 1 tbsp sherry vinegar; salt and freshly ground black pepper **METHOD** Bake the baguette slices in the oven (see page 61). Roast the mackerel fiercely at 230°C/450°F/Gas Mark 8 for 8–10 minutes. Skin and bone the cooled mackerel and set aside. Soften the leek and onion in the oil with the bay leaf. Add the wine and vinegar and poach for 8–10 minutes, allowing most of the liquid to evaporate. Remove and discard the bay leaf and season generously. Layer the toasted bread with the sautéed leek, mackerel and finally more leek.

LANGOSTINO GUACAMOLE (PRAWN AND GUACAMOLE TOASTS) makes 12 **INGREDIENTS** 1 baguette, sliced; oil, for brushing; 1 large, ripe avocado, roughly mashed; 1 large tomato, peeled, deseeded and diced; 1 spring onion, finely diced; 1 tsp chopped fresh coriander; salt and freshly ground black pepper; 3 medium potatoes, boiled and sliced in four; 125 ml (5 fl oz) garlic mayonnaise; 12 large prawns, cooked **METHOD** Bake the baguette slices in the oven (see page 61). To make the guacamole, mix the avocado, tomato, spring onion and coriander together. Season well. Coat the potatoes with the mayonnaise and place on the bread. Heap some guacamole on top and garnish with a prawn.

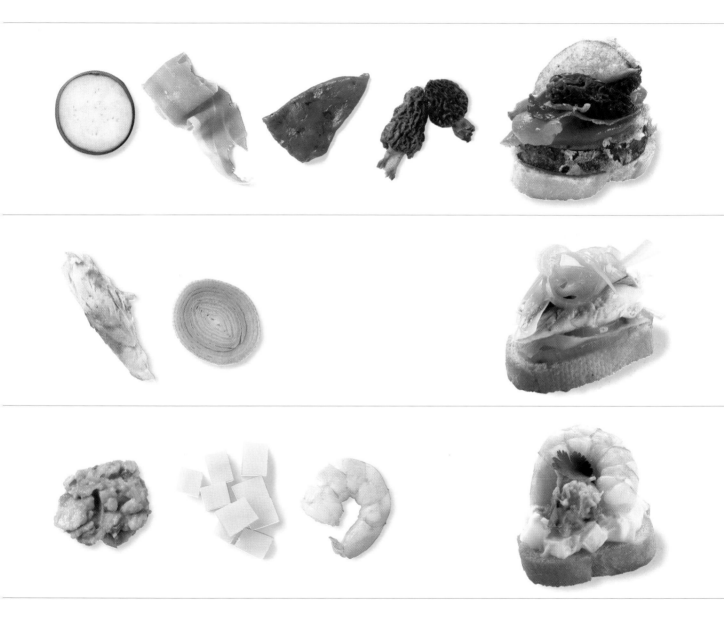

TOSTAS CON GARBANZOS Y PIMIENTOS (CHICKPEA AND PIMIENTO TOASTS)

Chickpeas, with their characteristically nutty flavour, are a staple of Middle Eastern and Mediterranean cuisine and were brought to Spain by the Moors. Tinned chickpeas are far quicker and easier to use then dried ones which need to be soaked overnight and boiled.

makes 12

INGREDIENTS

1 baguette

oil, for brushing

1 x 400 g (14 oz) tin chickpeas

2 tbsp olive oil

juice of 1 lemon

2 cloves garlic, crushed

2 tbsp chopped fresh parsley, plus
  extra for garnish

2 tsp hot smoked paprika

4 *pimientos de piquillo*, cut into strips

salt and freshly ground black pepper

EQUIPMENT

baking tray

METHOD

Slice the baguette into rounds about 1 cm (½ in) thick and brush with a little oil. Place on a baking tray and bake in the oven for about 5 minutes or until golden brown.

Drain the chickpeas and rinse under cold water; set aside. Place the oil, lemon juice and crushed garlic in a bowl and whisk together. Stir in the chopped parsley and paprika and then add the drained chickpeas and *pimiento* strips. Stir vigorously, crushing the chickpeas lightly so that they hold together. Place a spoonful of chickpea mixture onto each toast and serve immediately, garnished with parsley.

TARTALETAS

BARQUETA WALDORF

Puff pastry tartlets are a very useful substitute for toasted bread, not least because they are able to contain the rest of the ingredients more neatly and to much better effect. If you do not want to make your own pastry, use ready-made puff pastry, which is now conveniently available ready-rolled.

makes 12 tartlets

INGREDIENTS

250 g (9 oz) puff pastry (see page 75) or ½ packet of ready-made puff pastry

flour, for dusting

150 g (5 oz) *Cabrillanes*, Roquefort or other blue cheese

2 tbsp sour cream, crème fraîche or Greek yogurt

75 g (3 oz) walnuts, chopped

2 crisp red apples, cored and diced

1 stick celery, peeled and diced

4 leaves curly lettuce (e.g. lollo rosso)

EQUIPMENT

12 tartlet moulds

METHOD

Preheat the oven to 190°C/370°F/Gas Mark 5.

Roll the pastry out onto a floured board and use to line 12 tartlet moulds. Place in the oven and cook for about 5 minutes or until the pastry turns golden and starts to puff up. Remove from the oven and allow to cool.

Mash the cheese and cream together before adding the walnuts, apple and celery. Line the puff pastry container with a little of the lettuce and heap in the filling.

VARIATION: CURRIED TUNA makes 12 tartlets **INGREDIENTS** 1 medium onion, diced; 1 leek, diced; 2 tbsp light olive oil; 400 g (14 oz) tinned tuna; 100 ml (4 fl oz) cooking brandy; salt and freshly ground black pepper; 100 ml (4 fl oz) single cream; 2 tsp curry paste; 2 tbsp chopped fresh parsley **METHOD** Soften the onion and leek in the oil. Add the tuna and stir so it crumbles. Turn up the heat, add the brandy and carefully ignite with a match to flambé the tuna. When the flames have died down, season and set aside. Heat the cream and dissolve the curry paste in it. Add the cream to the tuna, return to the heat and cook through for 3–4 minutes, making sure you do not reduce the tuna to a pulp. Heap the tuna mixture into your puff pastry container, sprinkle with parsley and serve warm.

TARTALETA HONGOS Y JAMON (HAM AND MUSHROOM TARTLET)

Ham and mushrooms go well together. Cultivated "wild" mushrooms are readily available throughout most of the year.

makes 12 tartlets

INGREDIENTS

250 g (9 oz) puff pastry (see page 75)
   or ½ packet ready-made puff pastry

flour for dusting

1 tbsp light olive oil

1 tbsp shallots, finely diced

1 large clove garlic, crushed

250 g (9 oz) mixed wild mushrooms,
   chopped

100 g (3½ oz) *jamón*, diced

100 ml (4 fl oz) dry white wine

1 tbsp finely chopped fresh parsley

EQUIPMENT

frying pan

tartlet moulds

METHOD

Preheat the oven to 190°C/370°F/Gas Mark 5.

Roll the pastry out onto a floured board and use to line 12 tartlet moulds. Place in the oven and cook for about 5 minutes or until the pastry turns golden and starts to puff up. Remove from the oven and allow to cool.

Heat the oil in a frying pan and soften the shallots and garlic for 2–3 minutes. Add the mushrooms and *jamón*. After a minute or two, add the wine and bring up to a simmer for 7–8 minutes. Fill the tartlets, sprinkle over the parsley and serve.

TARTALETA DE SALMON, ESPARRAGOS Y ALCACHOFA (SALMON, ASPARAGUS AND ARTICHOKE TARTLET)

A ritzy tapa from the Hotel Europa in San Sebastian. It is a little time-consuming to put together, but the result is well worth the effort.

makes 12 tartlets

INGREDIENTS

250 g (9 oz) puff pastry (see page 75)
    or ½ packet ready-made puff pastry

flour for dusting

250 g (9 oz) salmon fillet, thinly sliced

1 tbsp sugar

1 tbsp salt

1 tbsp finely chopped fresh herbs,
    such as parsley, dill or chervil

200 g (7 oz) fine asparagus tips

100 g (3½ oz) tinned artichoke
    hearts

100 ml (4 fl oz) oil for frying

EQUIPMENT

1 heavy-based frying pan

tartlet moulds

METHOD

Preheat the oven to 190°C/370°F/Gas Mark 5.

Roll the pastry out onto a floured board and use to line 12 tartlet moulds. Place in the oven and cook for about 5 minutes or until the pastry turns golden and starts to puff up. Remove from the oven and allow to cool.

Place the salmon in the freezer for ½ hour to make it easier to slice thinly. Lay the slices out on a dish, sprinkle with sugar, salt and the herbs, cover and leave to marinate for 2 hours, turning once or twice. Brush the salmon clean with a pastry brush and set aside. Drop the asparagus into boiling salted water, bring back to the boil and simmer for 1½ minutes. Refresh in iced water, drain and set aside. Slice the artichokes finely and fry in the oil until crisp. Heat a heavy-based frying pan and sear the salmon for 30 seconds on each side. Place a slice of the salmon, then 2–3 asparagus tips, then an artichoke slice into the tartlet and serve.

TARTALETA DE BACALAO (SALT COD TARTLET)

Poaching in oil gives both the peppers and the fish a spectacular flavour and shaking the pan as it cooks releases the natural gelatin from the fish which makes the delicious sauce, known as *pil-pil*.

makes 12 tartlets

INGREDIENTS

250 g (9 oz) puff pastry (see page 75)
    or ½ packet ready-made puff pastry

flour for dusting

2 cloves garlic, crushed

2 red peppers, cut into broad strips

2 green peppers, cut into broad strips

175 ml (6 fl oz) light olive oil for frying

450 g (1 lb) *bacalao* (see page 13) or
    smoked haddock, skin on

salt and freshly ground black pepper

1 lemon, quartered

EQUIPMENT

frying pan

tartlet moulds

METHOD

Preheat the oven to 190°C/370°F/Gas Mark 5.

Roll the pastry out onto a floured board and use to line 12 tartlet moulds. Place in the oven and cook for about 5 minutes or until the pastry turns golden and starts to puff up. Remove from the oven and allow to cool.

Heat 2 tbsp of the oil in a frying pan and add the crushed garlic and the pepper strips. Gently cook the pepper strips until soft, about 10–12 minutes. Remove, allow to cool then peel, cut into narrow strips and set aside.

Add the remainder of the oil to the same pan. Place the fish, skin side down, very gently in the oil and poach for about 6 or 7 minutes, shaking the pan every few seconds towards the end to release the gelatin. Lift the fish out of the pan, remove the skin and bones and flake it. Fill the tartlets with fish, garnish with the pepper strips, season and daub with a little of the *pil-pil* sauce. Sprinkle over a little juice from the lemon wedges if you wish and serve.

BASIC RECIPES

SALSA ROSA

This "pink" sauce is a variation of prawn cocktail sauce and is great for serving with croquetas.

500 ml (18 fl oz) good-quality mayonnaise

1 tsp mustard

3 tbsp Worcester sauce

2 tbsp cognac

2 tbsp orange juice

1 tbsp (generous) tomato ketchup

3 tbsp single cream

salt and freshly ground black pepper

Place all the ingredients together in a bowl and mix well to combine.

VINAGRETA (Oil and vinegar dressing)

This is the Spanish for vinaigrette, the basic oil and vinegar dressing. Olive oil is most often used but you can substitute a lighter oil, if you prefer, or use a mixture of olive oil and sunflower oil. The Spanish like to customize their dressing by adding finely diced morsels, either to add a kick or a little bit of crunch – or sometimes just to add a bit of colour to the dressing.

200 ml (7 fl oz) olive oil

50 ml (2 fl oz) red wine vinegar

Salt and freshly ground black pepper

1 tbsp finely diced onion

1 tbsp finely diced spring onion

2 tsp finely diced *guindilla* chilli

2 tbsp finely chopped parsley

2 tbsp finely diced *pimientos de piquillo*

Whisk together the oil and vinegar in a bowl and season to taste. Whisk in any of the suggested additions, according to your preference. Do remember to keep the dice very fine.

PUFF PASTRY

Puff pastry can be tricky to master but if you are willing to have a go, you can produce a great result. The trick is to work in as cool an atmosphere as possible and not to let your fingers get too warm. If you are working the fat into the flour with your hands, run your hands under cold water first and dry thoroughly before starting.

225 g (8 oz) plain flour, sieved

pinch of salt

30 g (1 oz) lard

150 ml (1/4 pint) iced water

140 g (5 oz) butter

Place the sieved flour in a large bowl and mix in the salt. Work the lard into the flour with your fingers. When you have a mixture that resembles dry breadcrumbs, start adding the iced water. Mix with a knife until you achieve a dough that leaves the sides of the bowl cleanly and is quite elastic. Knead the dough until you have a smooth texture, turn it out, wrap it in clingfilm and leave it in the fridge to rest for half an hour.

Lightly flour a large wooden board or the table top and roll out the dough into a 10 x 30 cm (4 x 12 in) rectangle. Shape the butter into a flat block 9 cm (3 1/2 in) square.

Place the butter onto the pastry and bring the ends over to cover it. Fold the bottom third over, then the top third down. Press all the sides down to prevent the butter seeping out. Turn it ninety degrees anti-clockwise. The closed edge is now facing you.

Roll out the parcel quickly, so the pastry is three times longer than it is wide. Fold it exactly in three. The folded closed edge is now facing you. Press the edges down with your rolling pin. Roll out to form a rectangle as before.

Allow the pastry to rest for half an hour. It is then rolled and folded twice more, rested and then rolled and folded twice more. The pastry will have been "turned" six times. If you can see streaks of butter, you'll have to roll it and fold it again!

SUPPLIERS

UK

Pata Negra
tel: 020 8653 9628
fax: 020 8653 8504
email: mailorder@patanegra.net
www.patanegra.net
High quality Spanish food by mail order.

Brindisa
32 Exmouth Market
London EC1R 3LU
tel: 020 7713 1666
www.brindisa.com
Spanish delicatessen and wholesalers.

R Garcia & Sons
248-250 Portobello Road
London W11 1LL
tel/fax: 020 7221 6119
Spanish delicatessen and grocer.

Rias Altas
97 Frampton Street
London NW8 8NA
tel: 020 7262 4340
Spanish delicatessen. Also stocks
cooking implements.

Australia

Torres Cellars and Delicatessen
75 Liverpool St
Sydney, NSW 2000
tel: 02 9264-6862
fax: 02 9283-3242
email: deli@torres.com.au
www.torresdeli.com.au
Specialists in Spanish food and wine.

New Zealand

Bel Mondo
68 St John Street
Tauranga
tel: 07 579 0968
fax: 07 579 0969
Shop offering a wide selection of
Spanish and Mediterranean food,
incuding Italian, Greek, Turkish and
French products. Nationwide delivery
service.

South Africa

Thrupps
Illovo Centre
Corner Oxford and Rudd Roads
Illovo
Johannesburg
Tel: 011 788 2145
Fax: 011 880 1475
Thrupps grocery and specialist
departments offer a wide selection of
fine local and imported products.

Giovanni's Deliworld
103 Main Road
Green Point
Cape Town
Tel: 021 434 6893
Fax: 021 439 0348
Stocks a variety of oils, spice blends,
vinegars, meats and cheeses.

Ninadeli
10 Epsom Road
Stirling
East London
Eastern Cape
Tel: 043 735 3944
Fax: 043 735 4226
This deli offers a wonderful selection
of local and imported cheeses,
sausages, meats and fish.

Fab Deli
Juana Square
Smithfield
Free State
Tel/fax: 051 683 0516
The Fab Deli Stocks bottled olives,
capsicums, brinjals and meats.

Mr Mozzie's Smoke House
143 Stanford Hill Road
Umgeni
Durban
Tel: 031 309 1499
Fax: 031 309 1544
Stocks a wide variety of European
sausages and meat.

Many of the ingredients are available
at Spar outlets, Pick 'n Pay Food Halls
and Woolworths Foods countrywide.

INDEX